# A Note to

DK READERS is a compelling pr...... ......ing readers, designed in conjunction w..... ...ading literacy experts, including Dr. Linda Gambrell, Distinguished Professor of Education at Clemson University. Dr. Gambrell has served as President of the National Reading Conference, the College Reading Association, and the International Reading Association.

Beautiful illustrations and superb full-color photographs combine with engaging, easy-to-read stories to offer a fresh approach to each subject in the series. Each DK READER is guaranteed to capture a child's interest while developing his or her reading skills, general knowledge, and love of reading.

The five levels of DK READERS are aimed at different reading abilities, enabling you to choose the books that are exactly right for your child:

**Pre-level 1**: Learning to read
**Level 1**: Beginning to read
**Level 2**: Beginning to read alone
**Level 3**: Reading alone
**Level 4**: Proficient readers

The "normal" age at which a child begins to read can be anywhere from three to eight years old. Adult participation through the lower levels is very helpful for providing encouragement, discussing storylines, and sounding out unfamiliar words.

No matter which level you select, you can be sure that you are helping your child learn to read, then read to learn!

**DK** | Penguin Random House

**Project Editor** Penny Smith
**Designer** Andrew Burgess
**Series Editor** Deborah Lock
**Managing Art Editor** Martin Wilson
**US Editor** Regina Kahney
**Production Editor** Sarah Isle
**Picture Researcher** Jo Carlill
**Illustrator** Peter Dennis
**Jacket Designer** Natalie Godwin

**Reading Consultant**
Linda B. Gambrell, Ph.D.

First American Edition, 1998
This edition, 2012
16 10 9 8
Published in the United States by DK Publishing
345 Hudson Street, New York, New York 10014
009-185908-Feb/2012
Copyright © 1998 Dorling Kindersley Limited

Published in Great Britain by Dorling Kindersley Limited.

DK books are available at special discounts when purchased in bulk
for sales promotions, premiums, fund-raising, or educational use.
For details, contact: DK Publishing Special Markets
345 Hudson Street, New York, New York 10014
SpecialSales@dk.com

A catalog record for this book is available
from the Library of Congress

ISBN: 978-0-7566-9084-7 (pb)
ISBN: 978-0-7566-9085-4 (plc)

Color reproduction by Colourscan, Singapore
Printed and bound in China by L Rex Printing Co., Ltd.

The publisher would like to thank the following for their kind
permission to reproduce their photographs:
t=top, b=below, l=left, r=right, c=center,
BC=back cover, FC=front cover
Archive Photos: 3b, 4br, 18tr, 25, 47tr; Corbis-Bettmann: 9br, 22br,
30b; Finley Holiday Film Corporation: 7t;
Frank Spooner Pictures: 47br; Hulton Getty: 2cr, 26l, 36br;
Michael Freeman: 17tr, 24br, 34br, 40br; NASA: 1br, 5, 7br, 8t, 15,
16b, 20tr, 21, 28br, 31, 32br, 37c, 44b, 46t, 46b;
Rex Features: FC, 4tr, 27br, 29br, 32t, 33r, 45tr, 48br;
Robert Opie: 30b; Science Museum/Geoff Dann: FC;
Science Photo Library: 11, 36tr.
Additional photography by James Stevenson.
Jacket images: Front: NASA: StarBuzz.

All other images © Dorling Kindersley.
For further information see: www.dkimages.com

Discover more at
**www.dk.com**

# Contents

# DK READERS

READING **3** ALONE

# Spacebusters

## THE RACE TO THE MOON

In 1961 the President of the United States made a pledge that
America would send a man to the Moon before the end of the 1960s.
Here is the story of the final stage of that race against time.

## Written by Philip Wilkinson

DK Publishing

# Journey to the Moon

Three, two, one—blastoff! With a great roar the Apollo 11 rocket lifted off the ground. Flames and smoke poured from its base as it started its dangerous journey to the Moon.

President Kennedy had promised an American would reach the Moon before the end of the 1960s. It was already the summer of 1969. The astronauts could make history!

But Commander Neil Armstrong's heart pounded. He and his crew had only a fifty-fifty chance of returning alive.

**Takeoff, July 16, 1969**
The three astronauts were, from left to right, Neil Armstrong, Michael Collins, and Edwin Aldrin.

Armstrong kept an eye on the instrument panel. He watched the lights and dials change as the rocket quickly picked up speed.

Soon they were traveling 25,000 miles (40,200 kilometers) an hour—thirty times faster than a jet plane. The force pushed the men back into their seats and made it hard to move.

The entire spacecraft was taller than a skyscraper. Most of this was a rocket that held fuel. When the fuel was used up, the astronauts released the rocket and continued their journey in a capsule called the Command Module.

**Getting rid of the rocket**
After nearly 12 minutes the rocket, now empty of fuel, broke away and fell to the ground.

*Commander Neil Armstrong*

Armstrong turned to talk to Edwin Aldrin. It would take three days to reach the Moon, and Armstrong wanted to go over their planned landing.

Aldrin had spent years studying space. He looked forward to walking on the Moon and doing experiments there.

While Armstrong and Aldrin worked, the third astronaut, Michael Collins, got himself something to eat. Since everything in the spacecraft was weightless, ordinary food would float off a plate. Collins had to eat what looked like baby food from a plastic bag.

All the food had been dried to store it for the journey, so it had to be mixed with water. But there was plenty of choice, including beef and chicken.

**Space food**
Astronauts added water to dried food to make it sticky. This way no crumbs could float around and damage the spacecraft's controls.

As the spacecraft sped toward the Moon, the three men rested. They needed to save their energy so they would be wide awake for the dangers of the Moon landing ahead.

Out in space the Sun's heat is fierce. The capsule turned around and around. This stopped it from getting too hot on one side and burning up.

Sometimes when the men looked out the windows they could see the Earth. It was shining brightly and looked like a beautiful, giant disk in the sky.

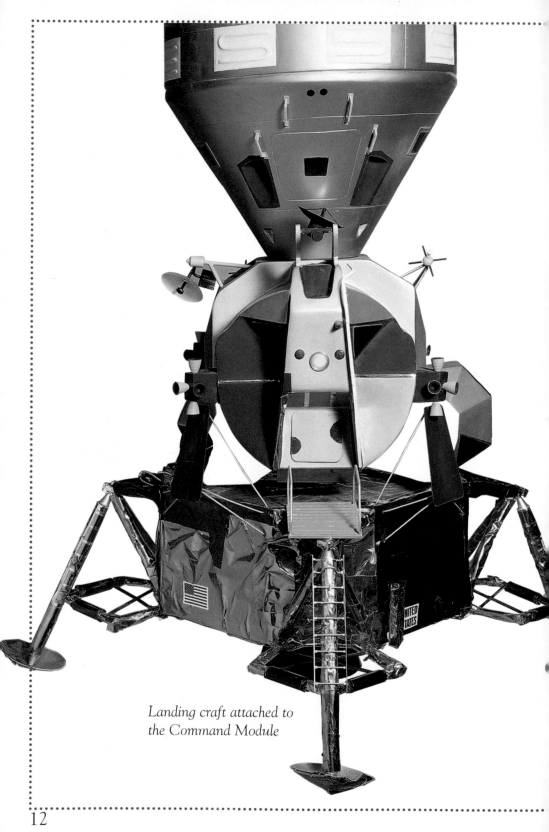

*Landing craft attached to
the Command Module*

The astronauts planned to set down on an area of the Moon called the Sea of Tranquility (tran-KWILL-it-ee). It was not a real sea because there is no water on the Moon.

From Earth, the Sea of Tranquility looked like a flat plain—a good surface to land on.

The spacecraft circled the Moon once, sending pictures back to Earth. Then the big moment arrived. It was time for two of the astronauts to try to land.

Armstrong and Aldrin prepared to leave the Command Module and enter the small landing craft that would take them to the Moon. They climbed through the craft's narrow hatch. The craft was nicknamed Eagle, but it looked more like a giant metal spider.

Collins stayed in the Command Module and pressed a button. Slowly the two crafts separated. Then the Eagle headed for the Moon's surface with its passengers on board.

As Armstrong and Aldrin drew close, they could see the surface more clearly.

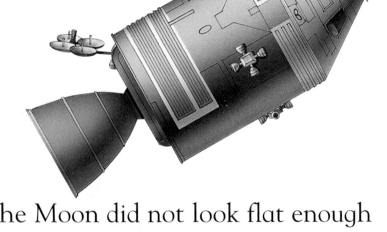

The Moon did not look flat enough to land on. It was peppered with craters and covered in boulders the size of small cars. They could not see a smooth place to set down!

The Eagle came closer and closer to the Moon. It was steered by a computer. But this computer couldn't see the dangerous surface ahead. It kept them straight on course. They were going to crash-land in a huge crater!

Armstrong grabbed the controls and began to fly the landing craft manually.

**Steering the landing craft**

Sixteen small rockets spaced around the landing craft were used to make the craft move right or left, up or down.

"How's the fuel?" he asked Aldrin.
"Eight percent," Aldrin replied.
This meant there was very little fuel left. They had only seconds to land!

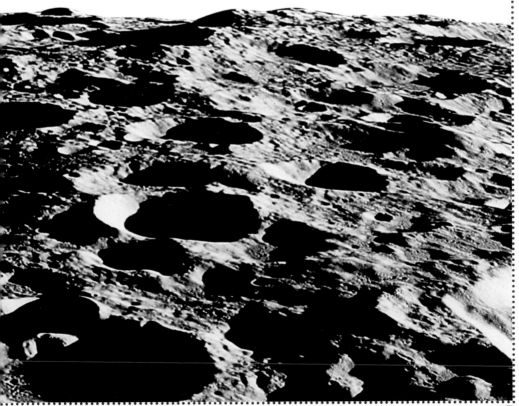

**Mission Control**
Scientists directed the flight from Mission Control in Texas. The person who spoke to the astronauts was called the CapCom.

Armstrong spotted a smooth place. Quickly he began to bring the craft straight down. Moon dust flew everywhere, and Armstrong could not see where they were going.

Then he heard Aldrin say, "Contact light." They were down! Armstrong hit the button marked "Engine Stop." Then he radioed Mission Control on Earth. "The Eagle has landed," he announced. ❖

# One giant leap

Neil Armstrong wanted to get out and explore the Moon right away. But he knew it was important to check the spacecraft first. He and Aldrin needed to make it ready for takeoff. If they met some unknown danger, they might have to leave the Moon in a hurry.

When the craft was ready, they helped each other put on their outside clothing. They pulled on overshoes. Then they put on helmets with visors to deflect the Sun's blinding light.

**Spacesuit**
A spacesuit is like a miniature spacecraft. It has everything the astronaut needs to survive outside the craft, such as a radio, oxygen, and watertight pouches to store urine. The astronauts can even sip drinks inside their suits.

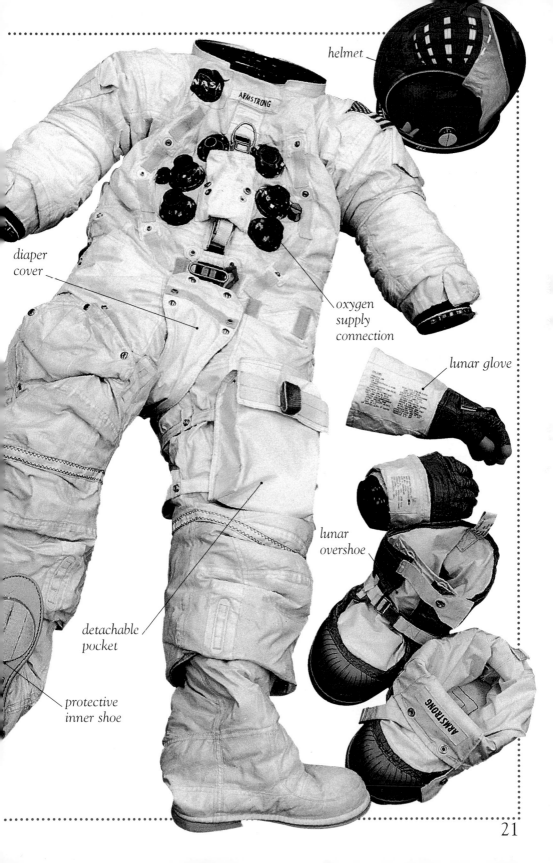

helmet

diaper
cover

oxygen
supply
connection

lunar glove

lunar
overshoe

detachable
pocket

protective
inner shoe

NASA

ARMSTRONG

ARMSTRONG

Each man also wore a huge backpack. It contained an oxygen supply so he could breathe. The packs were heavy, but everything is lighter on the Moon because there is less gravity, so the men could carry them with ease.

"All set for gloves?" Aldrin asked. Once these were on, the spacesuits were complete.

Then each man flicked a switch. Motors in the backpacks began to hum. Aldrin felt a whoosh on his face as oxygen filled his helmet. The men were ready to go outside.

**The force of gravity**
This force holds people on the ground. When people experience gravity weaker than it is on Earth, they feel lighter and can float.

Cameras in the landing craft sent pictures back to Mission Control on Earth. As the scientists watched, Armstrong pushed the hatch open and stepped through the gap.

Armstrong climbed carefully down the nine rungs toward the Moon's surface. He could see that the Moon was covered in a light dust. "It's almost like powder," he said into his radio to Mission Control. He hoped his feet would find firm ground.

Then he stepped off the last rung. Under the dust the ground was hard. Armstrong was elated. He was the first human being ever to stand on the Moon. His next words were heard all over the Earth. "That's one small step for man, one giant leap for mankind."

**Landing-craft feet**
The landing craft had wide feet to stop it from sinking into the Moon. Gold foil helped protect the feet from the cold.

Neil Armstrong looked over the bleak and barren landscape. Then he raised his camera and took some photographs.

*A scoop was used to collect rocks*

Next he bent over to collect samples for scientists on Earth. He filled a bag with dust, adding some rocks for good measure.

Armstrong was overjoyed. He had collected one bag of Moon samples. Now it was time for some fun. He threw away the handle of the collecting bag. Even with a gentle underarm throw, the handle traveled a long way. The Moon's gravity was too weak to pull it down.

Aldrin stayed in the landing craft. He watched his friend playing on the Moon's surface. "I didn't know you could throw so far," he joked.

**Moon rock**
This picture shows a slice of rock from the Moon. Some Moon rock is 4.6 billion years old.

Aldrin was itching to join Armstrong. At last it was his turn. Aldrin climbed slowly down the landing-craft ladder and stepped onto the Moon. He looked down. Wherever he put his boots, he left clear, sharp footprints.

Together Aldrin and Armstrong planted the American flag. It was hard to push the flag into the Moon's rough surface. But once it was up the men stood next to it and felt proud.

Then Aldrin decided to try running.

**Footprints**
There is no wind or rain on the Moon, so the astronauts' footprints will remain there forever.

He made huge strides and bounded like a kangaroo. But he felt as though he was running in slow motion.

*Aldrin stands next to the American flag, which was stiffened with wire because there is no wind on the Moon.*

The astronauts were having fun when Mission Control came on the radio. "The President of the United States would like to say a few words to you."

Armstrong and Aldrin pulled up short. They were so busy that they had forgotten people all over the world were watching them on television.

President Richard Nixon spoke briefly to the men. "All the people on this Earth are truly one," he said. "One in their pride in what you have done."

The astronauts got busy—there was work to be done! First they set up a machine that was able to detect any movements on the Moon's surface.

**Measuring instrument**
This showed that it's 240,000 miles (390,000 kilometers) from the Earth to the Moon. That's more than nine times around the world.

The machine would send this information back to Earth. They also set up an instrument to help scientists measure the distance from the Earth to the Moon.

The men worked for two and a half hours, then returned to the Eagle to rest. They had to be alert to take off and dock with the Command Module, which was orbiting the Moon. One mistake and they could drift off into space and be lost forever.

Armstrong and Aldrin climbed into the landing craft and closed the hatch. They were covered in Moon dust. Some scientists had said the dust would catch fire in oxygen. But the astronauts needed oxygen to breathe. They turned on the air supply and waited. The cabin filled with air. But the dust was safe. It did not ignite.

Then the men tried to rest, but they were too keyed up about liftoff. Collins was circling around the Moon. Would they ever see him again?

**Landing-craft engine**
One engine lifted the landing craft off the Moon. It fired for 7 minutes 45 seconds and took the astronauts into Moon orbit.

When it was finally time to leave the Moon, Aldrin hit the button marked "Proceed." The engine fired up. Moon dust and debris sprayed all around them. They were off! ❖

The landing craft left
its legs behind at takeoff

# Homeward bound

While Armstrong and Aldrin were exploring, Collins circled the Moon in the Command Module. For half of each orbit he was on the far side of the Moon—the side always turned away from the Earth. Everything was silent. No radio signals could reach him. Collins was completely out of contact with the rest of the human race. No one had ever been more alone.

Collins was worried that Armstrong and Aldrin would get stuck on the Moon, or that they wouldn't be able to dock with the Command Module. If either happened, he would have to leave his two friends to die in space.

*The Command Module orbiting the Moon*

At last, through his window, Collins spotted the landing craft coming toward him. He steered the Command Module carefully so that the two crafts lined up ready for docking.

The spacecrafts were almost touching. One false move and they could miss each other completely.

Seconds seemed liked hours. Then a buzzer sounded, and a set of latches closed with a clunk. The landing craft had attached to the Command Module.

Armstrong and Aldrin clambered back into the module. At last Collins could relax. They could all return to Earth together.

It would take three days for the astronauts to reach Earth. They caught up on their sleep on the long journey home.

At last, they entered the Earth's atmosphere—the layer of air around the planet. Then the outside of the spacecraft began to heat up. It became 25 times hotter than a kitchen oven.

The spacecraft was protected by a heat shield. Through the window, the astronauts could see bits of the shield come off and fly past them. They prayed that the shield would hold out.

**Heat shield**
Metals light enough for a spacecraft could not resist great heat. So the craft was coated with resin that would burn away and keep it cool.

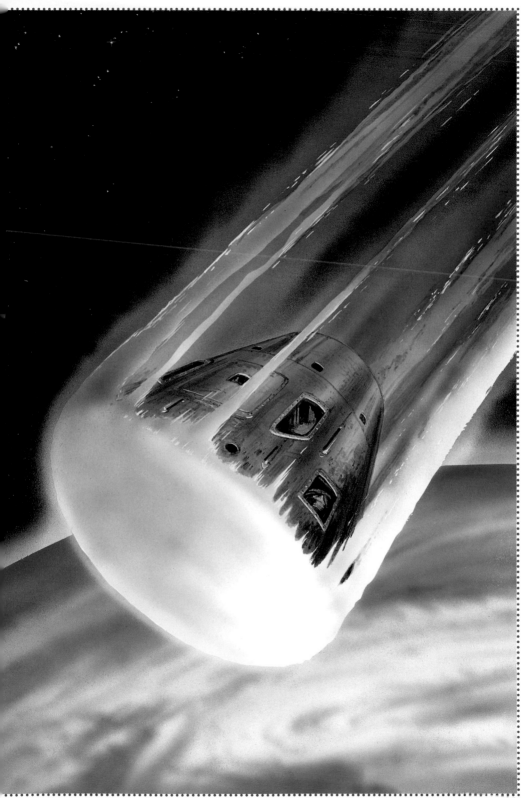

Crack! The astronauts heard the noise of the first small parachutes, called the drogues (DROGES), opening above them. The drogues set the craft on an even keel, so that it would fall steadily down to Earth.

Whoosh! A small vent opened, bringing air into the cabin. This made the air inside the craft the same as it was on the outside.

Then there was another cracking sound. "There go the mains," said Armstrong. He meant the main parachutes. Now they were floating slowly down. Finally, with a loud splash, they landed in the Pacific Ocean.

The pick-up crew found them floating there several minutes later. They seemed fine, but what if they had brought back new germs from the Moon? Swimmers threw germproof rubber suits to the astronauts, and the men put them on. It was best not to take any chances.

Back on land, the astronauts had to be kept apart from other people until they had been thoroughly tested. The three men had to spend about two weeks locked in a special laboratory.

Only their doctors were supposed to go in with them. But some of the scientists had touched the Moon  rock samples by accident, and they had to stay in the lab too.

Then one hot evening the doctors said the astronauts were all in good health. The men were let out of the small room at last, free to go home to their wives and children. ❖

# The later years

After Apollo 11 there were six more Apollo missions to the Moon. Some of the astronauts on these missions explored the Moon using a small, battery-powered car called a Lunar Rover.

In 1981 a new spacecraft blasted off—the Space Shuttle. Unlike the Apollo rockets, the Shuttle was reusable. Its huge cargo hold carried scientific equipment into space to do work that would be impossible to do on Earth.

*Neil Armstrong became a director of the Space Agency in Washington, D.C. He later retired to run a farm in his native Ohio.*